MY MINI CONCERT
MUSICAL INSTRUMENTS FOR KIDS

MUSIC BOOK FOR BEGINNERS
CHILDREN'S MUSICAL INSTRUMENTS

In this book we're going to talk about the different types of musical instruments. So lets get right to it!

There are four main types of musical instruments. The categories are string, brass, percussion and woodwinds. Not every instrument fits into these four categories but most do.

STRING INSTRUMENTS

STRINGS PLUCKED

STRINGS BOW

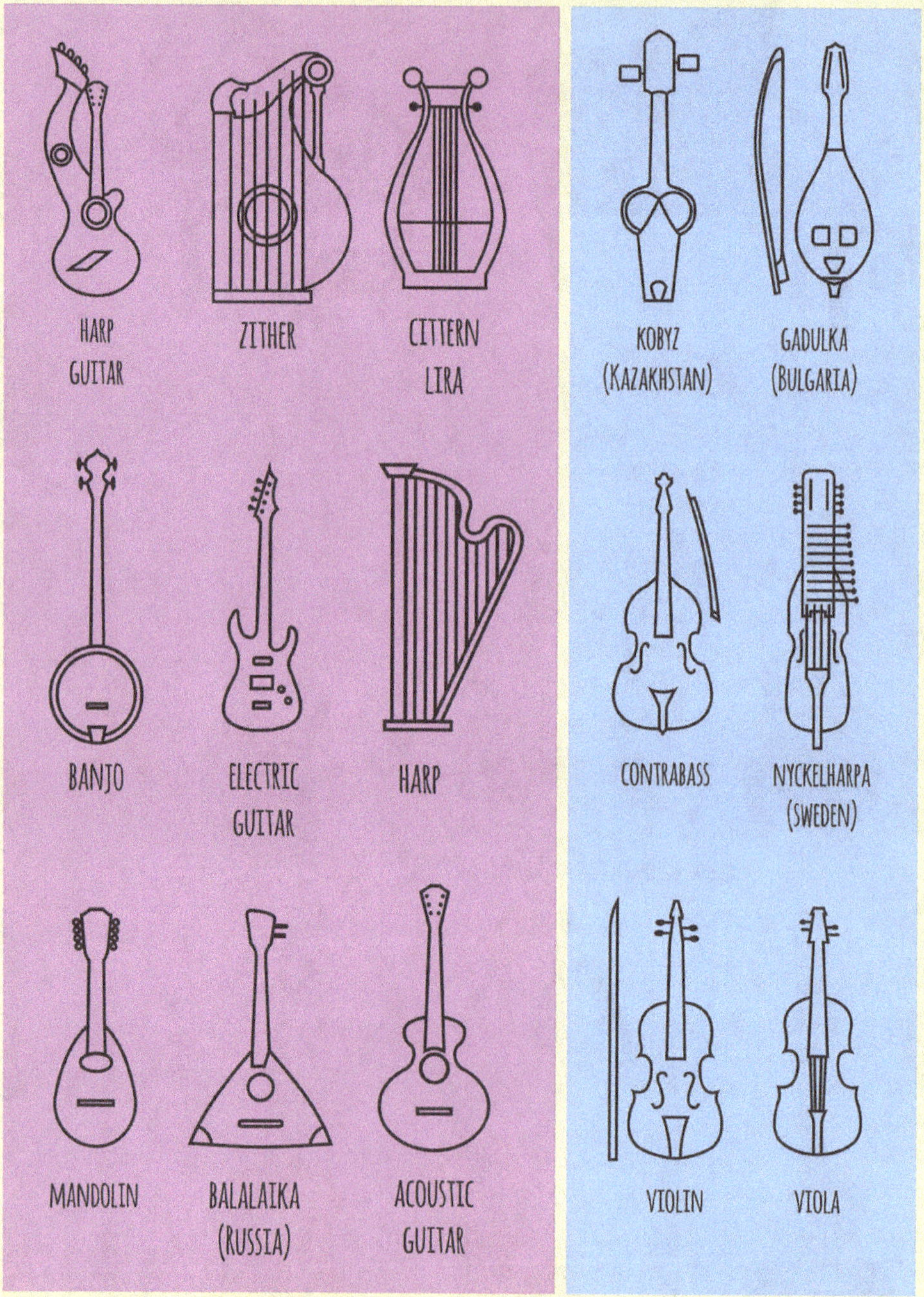

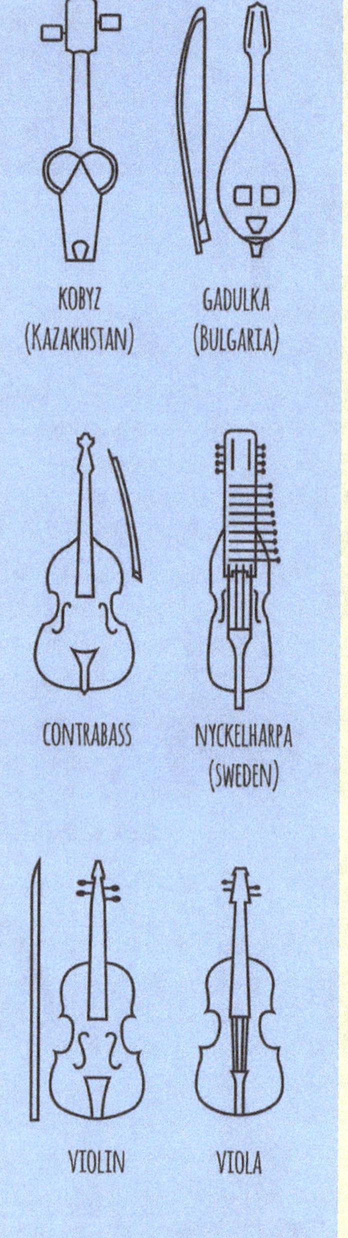

STRING INSTRUMENTS

String instruments have been used to play music for thousands of years. Artwork from ancient Egypt depicts the Egyptians playing music on the harp around 3000 BCE. The Old Testament mentions the harp as well as the lyre in many passages.

In ancient Greece Pythagoras, the mathematician that derived the now famous Pythagorean theorem, made an important discovery. He found out that if strings were in a

PYTHAGORAS

certain proportional relationship with each other in terms of their length then the sounds they made when plucked at the same time were harmonious. In other words if one string was twice the length of the other then when they were both plucked the music they made was harmonious.

STRING INSTRUMENTS

There are hundreds of different types of string instruments. An orchestra will have violins, violas, cellos, double basses and a harp. A contemporary group might have guitars or banjos. Every type of string instrument has a unique sound.

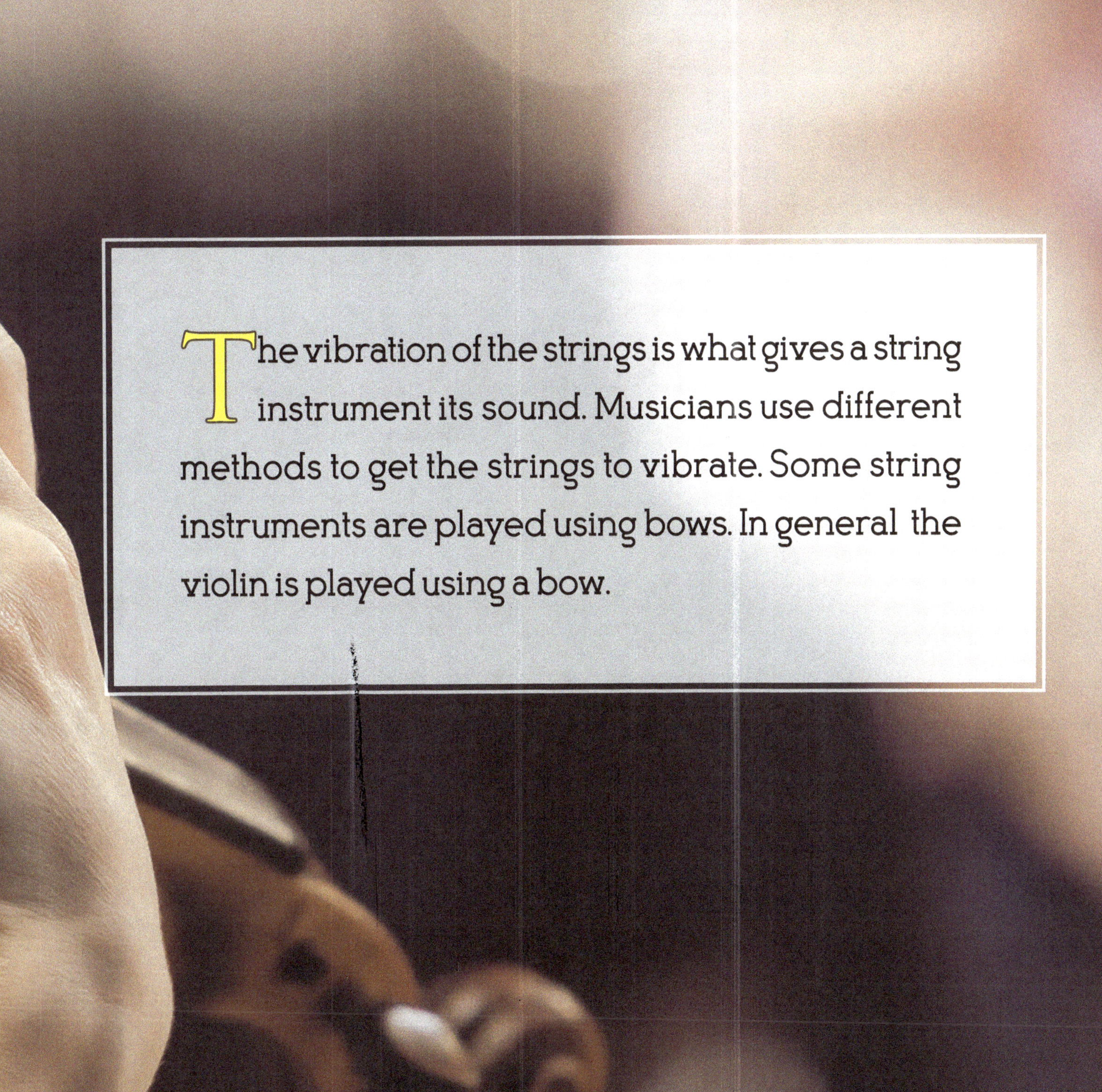

The vibration of the strings is what gives a string instrument its sound. Musicians use different methods to get the strings to vibrate. Some string instruments are played using bows. In general the violin is played using a bow.

Other string instruments are played with picks or with the musicians fingers. For example a musician can use his fingers or a pick to strum the strings of a guitar.

A guitar's strings can be plucked to make a sound that is different than the sound of strumming.

There are three different factors that determine the sound of the notes a string produces.

LENGTH

Shorter strings make higher notes than longer strings do. When you see a guitarist strum the strings with one hand and press down on the strings with the other they are controlling the length of the strings which changes the sound.

A HARP IS PLAYED WITH BOTH HANDS

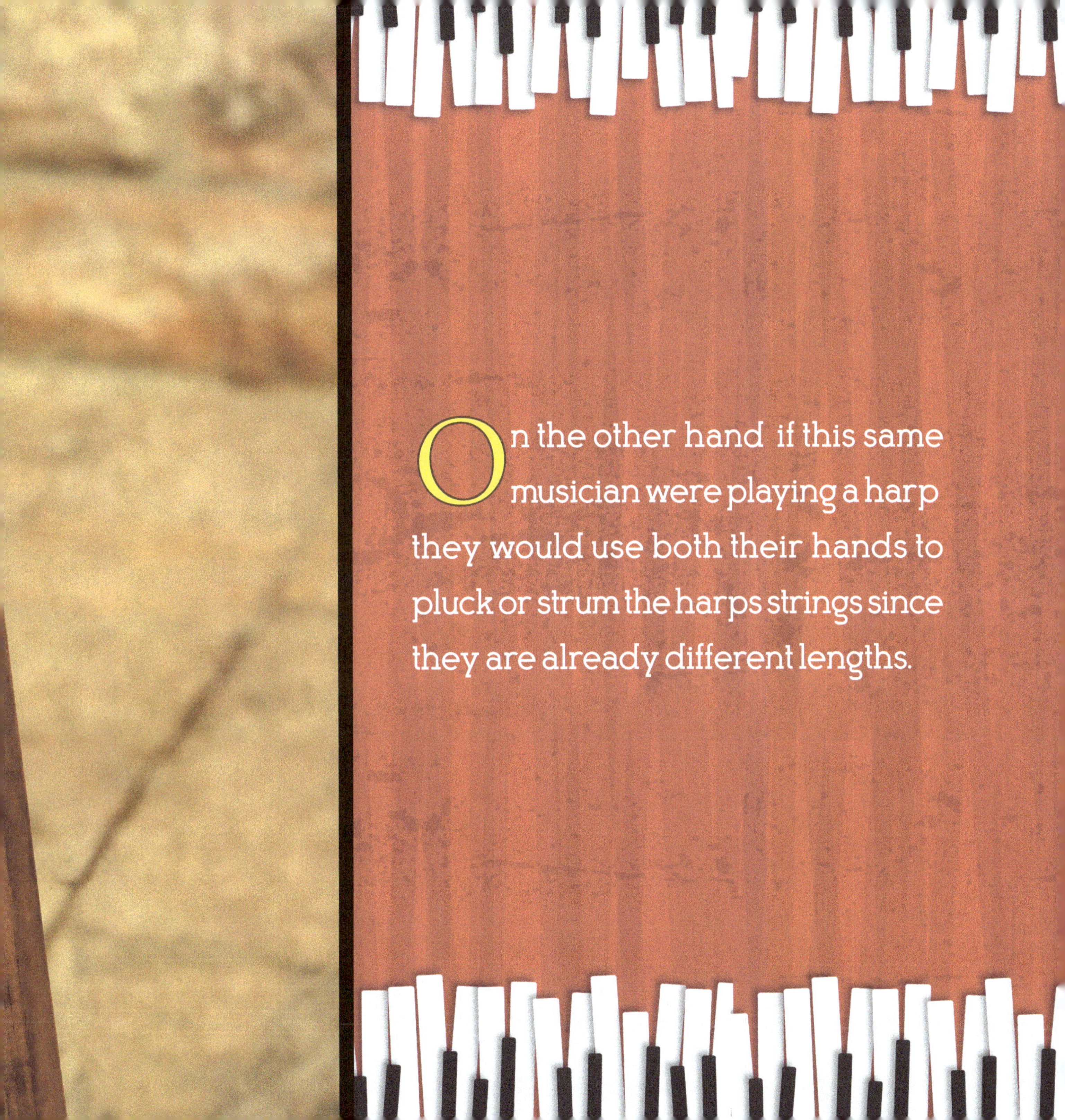

On the other hand if this same musician were playing a harp they would use both their hands to pluck or strum the harps strings since they are already different lengths.

WEIGHT

If a string is very thick or heavy then it will make a low sounding note compared to a lightweight thinner string.

TIGHTNESS

The tighter a string, the higher the note it will produce.

The string isn't the only thing that creates the sound that comes from a string instrument. By itself the string doesn't make a sound that's very loud or very musical. It's the body of the instrument that helps the sounds from the strings work.

GUZHENG
A CHINESE PLUCKED STRING INSTRUMENT

The instruments body makes the sound louder which is called amplification. The body acts as a soundbox also called a resonator.

The top of the resonator is usually constructed from a piece of wood that also vibrates. This wood piece is called the soundboard.

For example when you play the guitar you strum or pluck the strings. The vibrations are then carried by the bridge since the strings are positioned on the bridge. The soundboard begins to vibrate from the vibrations on the bridge and the soundbox amplifies the sound so it's loud enough for people to hear.

Because of the different woods and other materials used in guitars, violins and other string instruments the sound will be different.

In fact there are some violins such as Stradivarius violins that are worth millions of dollars due to their unique rich sound.

BRASS INSTRUMENTS

Brass instruments make bright focused sounds that are often very loud. There are many different types of brass instruments such as the trombone, the trumpet, the cornet and the tuba. The tuba makes the lowest notes of all the brass instruments.

WIND BRASS

TRUMPETS

SAXOPHONE

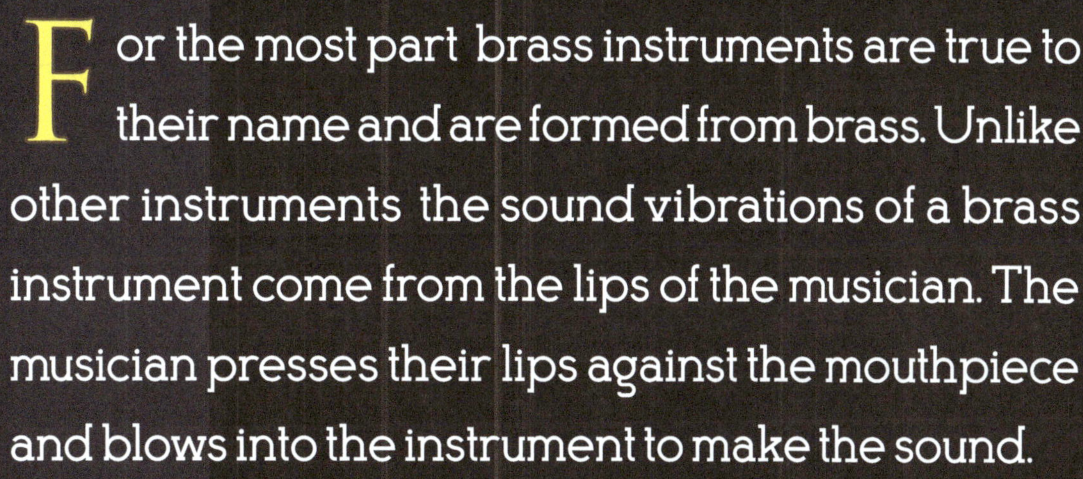

For the most part brass instruments are true to their name and are formed from brass. Unlike other instruments the sound vibrations of a brass instrument come from the lips of the musician. The musician presses their lips against the mouthpiece and blows into the instrument to make the sound.

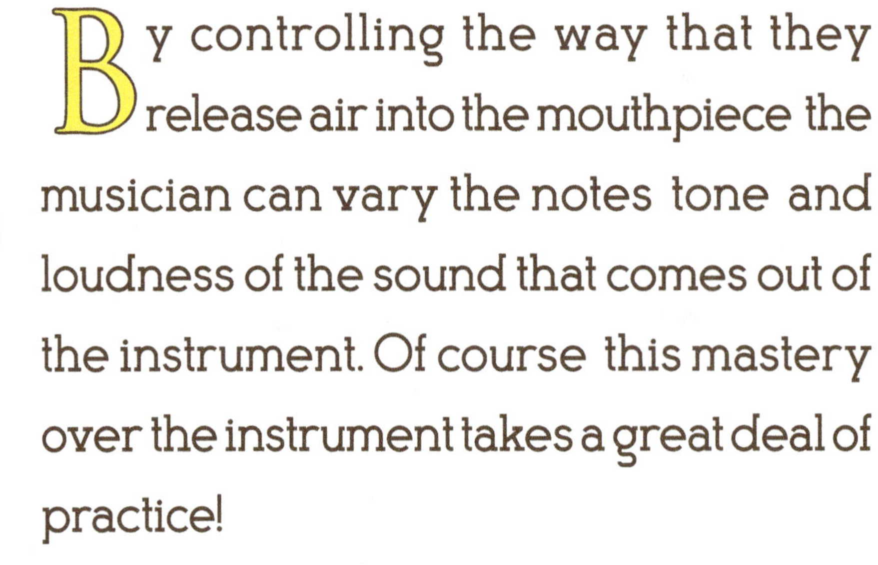

By controlling the way that they release air into the mouthpiece the musician can vary the notes tone and loudness of the sound that comes out of the instrument. Of course this mastery over the instrument takes a great deal of practice!

The horns body makes the sound louder and creates the various notes. The tubular section of the instrument is described as the bore and the end portion that flares out is described as the bell.

FRENCH HORN

Trumpet

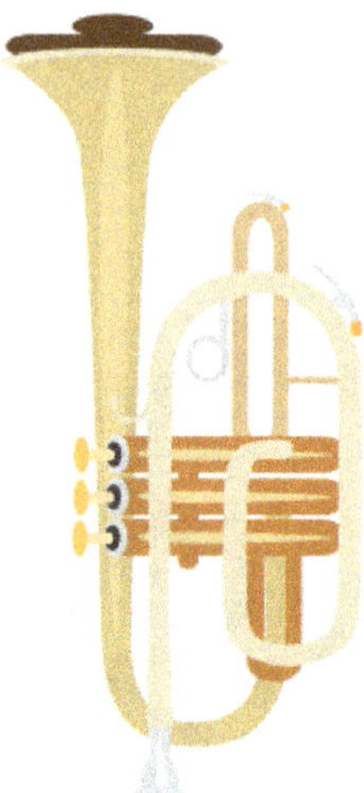

Trumpet

Clarinet

Trombone

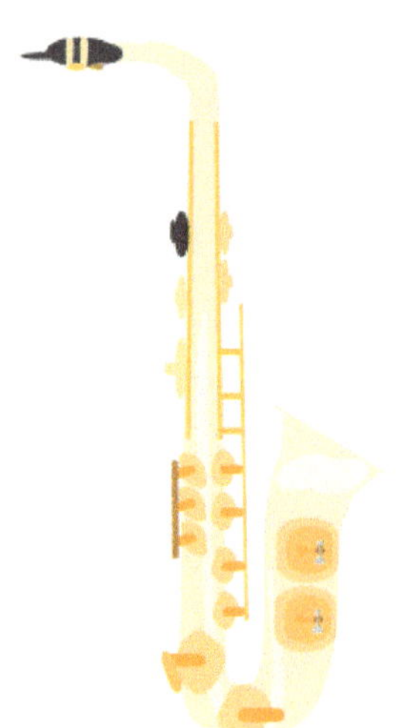

Saxophone

French horn

Tuba

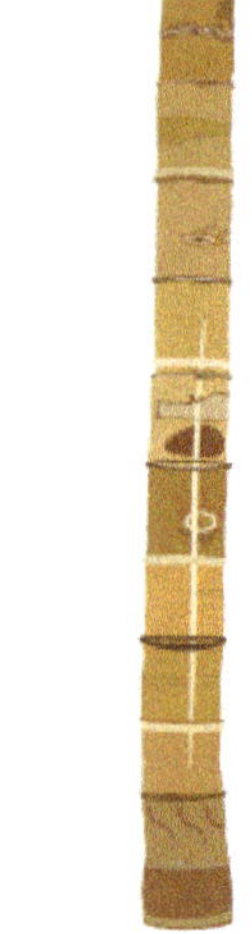

Didgeridoo

The instruments tone is largely controlled by the bores general shape, its overall length and its width. These differences are what make a trumpet's sound sharp and blaring and a French horn's sound mellow and rich.

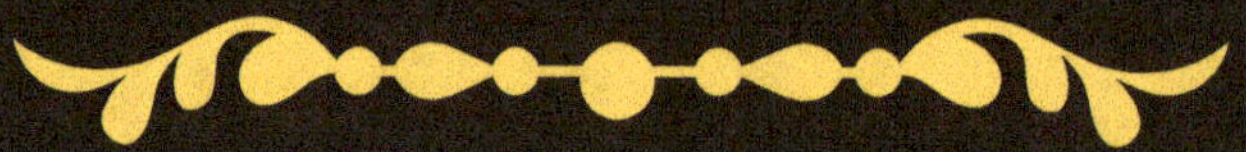

For a very long time throughout history horns were a specific length and as a result they couldn't make a wide range of notes. However in the 15th century slides were introduced and several centuries later valves were invented. These innovations made it possible for the musician to alter the tubes length thereby changing the sound.

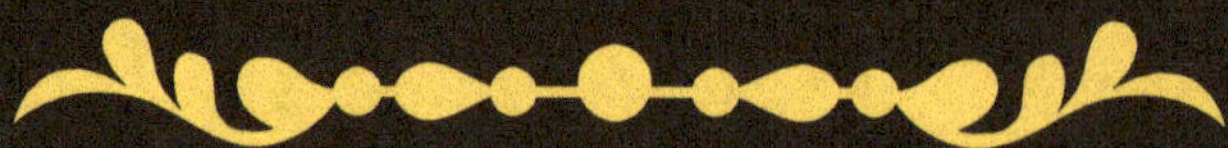

FRENCH HORN PLAYER

For example on a trombone the slide allows the musician to change the length of the tube and smoothly slide between two different notes. If a musician wants to change a note quickly he or she would use the valves.

Valves can be used by themselves or in conjunction with other valves. When the valves are pressed down it forces the stream of air into a greater length of tubing. This lowers the tone being produced.

Brass instruments are used in many different types of music. Big bands and symphony orchestras both use brass instruments. They're popular for use in marching bands since they are so loud they can be heard without additional amplifiers.

TRADITIONAL WOODWIND INSTRUMENTS

WOODWIND INSTRUMENTS

W oodwind instruments are sometimes made of wood but today many are made out of hard plastic or various types of metal. Smaller instruments make higher pitch sounds than bigger longer instruments do. There are two actions that work in tandem so that woodwind instruments can create sound. The musician blows air into them and then controls whether holes in the instrument are opened or closed to create the various notes.

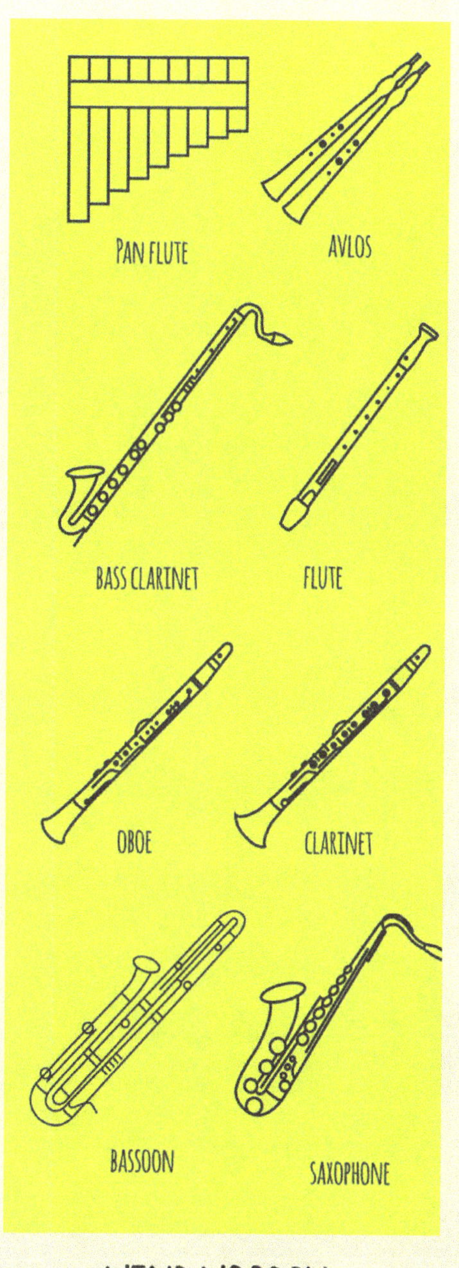

WIND WOODEN

Woodwind instruments belong to two different families, flutes or reeds. When a musician plays a flute he or she blows air over an edge that is located at the beginning of the mouthpiece or deeper inside the mouthpiece. The air separates causing vibrations. The flute, the fife and the piccolo are examples of instruments in the flute family.

WOODWIND INSTRUMENTS

With reed instruments when the musician blows air through the mouthpiece it hits a narrow piece of wood described as a reed. As the reed begins to vibrate it creates sound. For example the clarinet as well as the saxophone are instruments that have just one reed.

There are also reed instruments that have two reeds that vibrate. The oboe has two reeds and so does the bassoon.

The holes in a woodwind instrument are covered with the musicians fingers. Some instruments like the saxophone have keys that the musician presses to cover the holes.

PERCUSSION INSTRUMENTS

Perhaps the very first instrument you ever played was a toy drum. Drums and cymbals are percussion instruments. Percussion instruments create sounds when you hit them or scrape them with a separate object or with your fingers.

Percussion Instruments

Some types of percussion instruments like castanets make sounds when you shake them. There are hundreds of different types of percussion instruments and they create the beat of the music.

Unlike other musicians in an orchestra a percussionist may be responsible for playing several different instruments throughout the performance of a symphony.

PIANO

The piano is one of the most popular musical instruments around the world. The piano has some characteristics of a string instrument and some of a percussion instrument so it's in a category of its own.

A standard piano has over 200 strings although it only has 88 keys each of which plays a specific note. The reason is that some of the higher notes require 3 strings and some of the notes that are lower require 2 strings.

PIANO

When a pianist hits a key on the piano a small piece described as a hammer strikes a string or a set of strings. The string vibrates to create the sounds of a designated note.

Under the strings is a soundboard which helps to make the sound louder and gives the piano its unique tone.

SUMMARY

Most musical instruments fall into four major categories. They can be classified as either string, brass, woodwind or percussion instruments. However there are some instruments that can't be categorized this way. The piano is a very popular instrument that has vibrating strings like a string instrument. However unlike a string instrument its strings vibrate once the pianist touches the keys. In a way it's a cross between a string instrument and a percussion instrument.

DIFFERENT MUSICAL
INSTRUMENTS

Now that you've read about different types of musical instruments you may want to read about how music and entertainment helped people during the Great Depression in the Baby Professor book The Great Depression Wasn't Always Sad! Entertainment and Jazz Music Book for Kids Childrens Arts Music   Photography Books.

Visit

www.BabyProfessorBooks.com

to download Free Baby Professor eBooks
and view our catalog of new and exciting
Children's Books

9 798869 437174